Hon and Honey

by Lola M. Schaefer

Consulting Editor: Gail Saunders-Smith, Ph.D.

Consultant: Troy Fore, Executive Director,
American Beekeeping Federation

an imprint of Capstone Press
Mankato, Minnesota

1

Pebble Books are published by Capstone Press
818 North Willow Street, Mankato, Minnesota 56001
http://www.capstone-press.com

Library of Congress Cataloging-in-Publication Data
Schaefer, Lola M., 1950–
    Honey bees and honey /by Lola M. Schaefer.
      p. cm.—(Honey bees)
    Includes bibliographical references and index.
    Summary: Simple text and photographs describe how honeybees make and
beekeepers collect honey.
      ISBN 0-7368-0233-9
      1. Honeybee—Juvenile literature. 2. Honey—Juvenile literature. [1. Honeybee.
2. Bees. 3. Honey.] I. Title. II. Series: Schaefer, Lola M., 1950–   Honey bees.
QL568.A6S284   1999
595.79′9—dc21   98-40906
                                                                                        CIP
                                                                                        AC

Note to Parents and Teachers

The Honey Bees series supports national science standards for units
on the diversity and unity of life. The series also shows that animals
have features that help them live in different environments. This
book describes and illustrates how honey bees make honey. The
photographs support early readers in understanding the text. The
repetition of words and phrases helps early readers learn new
words. This book also introduces early readers to subject-specific
vocabulary words, which are defined in the Words to Know section.
Early readers may need assistance to read some words and to use
the Table of Contents, Words to Know, Read More, Internet Sites,
and Index/Word List sections of the book.

2

Table of Contents

Honey bees make honey in hives.

Honey bees build
honeycombs in hives.

Honey bees gather nectar from flowers.

Honey bees carry nectar to their hives.

12

Honey bees put nectar
in the honeycombs.

Honey bees dry nectar until it ripens into honey.

Honey bees eat some
of the honey.

Beekeepers gather some of the honey.

Honey sweetens food.

Words to Know

beekeeper—a person who raises honey bees and gathers honey from their hives

hive—a structure where honey bees live; thousands of honey bees live in a hive.

honey—a sweet, sticky matter that honey bees make from nectar; chemicals in honey bee saliva help dry nectar; honey bees also beat their wings to dry nectar.

honeycomb—a group of wax cells built by honey bees in their hive; honey bees store pollen, nectar, honey, and eggs in the cells.

nectar—a sweet liquid that honey bees gather from flowers; honey bees gather nectar from about 2 million flowers to make 1 pound (.5 kilograms) of honey.

ripen—ready to be harvested, picked, or eaten; honey bees dry nectar until it ripens into honey.

sweeten—to make something sweet or sweeter

Read More

Gibbons, Gail. *The Honey Makers.* New York: Morrow Junior Books, 1997.

Holmes, Kevin J. *Bees.* Animals. Mankato, Minn.: Bridgestone Books, 1998.

Micucci, Charles. *The Life and Times of the Honeybee.* New York: Ticknor & Fields, 1995.

Internet Sites

The Honey Expert
http://www.honey.com

Honey Glossary
http://www.honey.com/kids/gloss.html

Making the Honey
http://honeybee.com.au/making.html

Index/Word List

Word Count: 57
Early-Intervention Level: 9

Editorial Credits
Martha E. Hillman, editor; Steve Weil/Tandem Design, cover designer and
    illustrator; Kimberly Danger, photo researcher

Photo Credits
Craig D. Wood, cover, 4, 16
K. D. Dittlinger, 20
Lynn M. Stone, 18
McDaniel Photography/Stephen McDaniel, 8, 10
Photo Network/D & I MacDonald, 1
Scott Camazine, 6, 12, 14